Did

BOURN

A MISCELLANY

Compiled by Julia Skinner

With particular reference to the work of John Bainbridge

THE FRANCIS FRITH COLLECTION

www.francisfrith.com

Based on a book first published in the United Kingdom in 2005 by The Francis Frith Collection®

This edition published exclusively for Identity Books in 2011 ISBN 978-1-84589-427-6

Text and Design copyright The Francis Frith Collection®
Photographs copyright The Francis Frith Collection® except where indicated.

The Frith® photographs and the Frith® logo are reproduced under licence from
Heritage Photographic Resources Ltd, the owners of the Frith® archive and trademarks.
'The Francis Frith Collection', 'Francis Frith' and 'Frith' are registered trademarks of
Heritage Photographic Resources Ltd.

British Library Cataloguing in Publication Data

Did You Know? Bournemouth - A Miscellany
Compiled by Julia Skinner
With particular reference to the work of John Bainbridge

The Francis Frith Collection
Oakley Business Park, Wylie Road,
Dinton, Wiltshire SP3 5EU
Tel: +44 (0) 1722 716 376
Email: info@francisfrith.co.uk
www.francisfrith.com

Printed and bound in Malaysia

Front Cover: **BOURNEMOUTH, THE GARDENS 1922** 72700p

The colour-tinting is for illustrative purposes only, and is not intended to be historically accurate

CONTENTS

INTRODUCTION

Bournemouth, once in Hampshire but now in Dorset, did not exist at all until Captain Lewis Tregonwell built a holiday home in the middle of empty heathland, on the site of what is now the Royal Exeter Hotel. At that time (1810-11), Tregonwell's house was the only building, apart from an inn, on a wild stretch of coastline frequented only by fishermen, turf cutters and smugglers. The area was described in 1805 as a 'most dreary waste, serving only in the summer to support a few ordinary sheep and cattle, and to supply the neighbouring villages with firing'.

During the 19th century Bournemouth was developed as a select resort for the well-off and its mild climate made it popular with invalids, particularly those suffering from tuberculosis, the scourge of the 19th and early 20th centuries. The town's status as a fashionable resort was confirmed when Queen Victoria recommended it to Disraeli, who stayed there for three months to alleviate his gout. Much of the credit for the popularity of Bournemouth can be given to Sir Merton Russell-Cotes and his wife, Annie, who promoted the resort tirelessly, and campaigned for the promenade to be built along the seafront.

In the 20th century Bournemouth opened its beaches to all, and became one of England's most popular holiday destinations, 'the Queen of the South'. At the end of the 20th century Bournemouth not only maintained its reputation as a leading resort, with excellent shopping and entertainment facilities, but also developed as a first-class conference venue, and became a university town - from holiday home to all this in less than 200 years!

Bournemouth's story is full of colourful characters and events, of which this book can only give a glimpse.

SOUTHBOURNE, FISHERMAN'S WALK 1908 61204

LITERARY BOURNEMOUTH

Mary Shelley, creator of 'Frankenstein', lived in Bournemouth for many years and is buried in St Peter's churchyard, alongside the heart of her husband, the poet Percy Bysshe Shelley. Their son, Percy Florence Shelley, had associations with Boscombe.

Robert Louis Stevenson came to Bournemouth to benefit his health, and wrote 'Kidnapped' and 'Dr Jekyll and Mr Hyde' whilst in the town. The house he stayed in, Skerryvore, at the corner of Alum Chine Road and Robert Louis Stevenson Avenue in Westbourne, was damaged in the Second World War and had to be demolished, but a memorial plaque marks the site.

Thomas Hardy described the town as 'Sandbourne' in his novel 'The Hand of Ethelberta', and immortalised it in 'Tess of the d'Urbervilles' as 'the city of detached mansions'.

BOURNEMOUTH, THE PIER 1897 40559

HAUNTED BOURNEMOUTH

Bournemouth's Town Hall is reputedly haunted by the ghost of a soldier from the First World War. He appears there once a year on 31 October to help himself to a drink of water. Rooms in the Town Hall are also said to be haunted by a ghostly cat, and phantom horses and carriages have been seen outside the building, which used to be a luxury hotel in the 19th century.

Talbot Woods are apparently haunted by a very large dog. It has never been seen directly, but only as a shadowy form just out of vision; witnesses have also reported hearing scraping sounds, as of claws.

The area around the bridge in Millhams Lane, in the Longham area, is haunted by the ghost of a white lady. She is believed to have been killed by a horse and trap whilst walking along the road. Some stories say that she tries to entice men to jump off the bridge.

In the 1980s there was a report of a ghostly sighting in the Gulliver's pub, then known as the Dolphin, in Kinson. The witnesses were woken in the night by the sound of clinking; on investigation, they saw what appeared to be a man sitting on a chest, counting out gold coins. The story was no doubt linked to Kinson's connections with smuggling. The ghosts of local smugglers are also said to haunt the area around St Andrew's Church.

BOURNEMOUTH MISCELLANY

Bournemouth's original pleasure gardens, created in what were Westover Plantations in 1858, were laid out below a wide path named Invalid's Walk. The wealthy infirm at that time provided the main clientele for seaside resorts in southern England. Harry Furniss wrote in the journal 'Good Words' in 1891: 'The place exists chiefly for the invalid'. It was not until after the First World War that the name of the walk was changed to Pine Walk.

When Lady Meyrick officially opened the electrically-powered East Cliff railway lift in 1908 (see right), her husband confided his hope that they would not have to use it!

Charles Darwin stayed at Cliff Cottage on South Cliff Road in 1862 while his wife recuperated from scarlet fever. He described the heathlands around Bournemouth as 'nice but barren'. Brooks and ponds were lifeless, and he complained that 'the country is like Patagonia'. Cliff Cottage was demolished in 1876, and its site is now absorbed into Bournemouth International Centre.

Bournemouth Pier stands above the original mouth of the River Bourne. Its construction marked the town's commitment to its role as a resort. The mildness of the climate first attracted visitors to the town, and it rapidly acquired a reputation as a place beneficial to consumptives (those suffering from tuberculosis).

SOUTHBOURNE, THE CLIFF RAILWAY c1955   S153115

7

BOURNEMOUTH, THE SQUARE 1904 52875

Electric trams began running in Bournemouth on 23 July 1902, although they were eventually given up in favour of electric trolleybuses. The old tramlines were eventually torn up and used to reinforce the concrete of the sea wall.

In the photograph on page 9, Undercliff Drive has not yet been built. There are bathing machines along the beach, and a paddle-steamer is reversing away from the pier-head. It is probably setting off for Swanage, the Isle of Wight, or for France. There was lively competition between the 'Balmoral' from Southampton and the 'Majestic' from Weymouth for the fastest run from Bournemouth to Cherbourg (France) and back; the eventual record was established by the 'Balmoral' on 20 July 1908, with a time of 3 hours and 37 minutes each way.

Unlike older resorts, which had grown up around existing industries such as fishing and merchant shipping, Bournemouth was designed from the start as a venue for holiday pleasures, spurred on by the enterprising Sir George Tapps-Gervis, a wealthy landowner. He saw the potential of the area as a resort, and in 1837 Westover Villas, Westover Gardens and the Bath Hotel were built. Under his guidance the first real hotels began to appear, a library and reading room were established, and the first villas - available for hire at four guineas a week - began to line the cliff tops. An early travel writer said: 'The magic hand of enterprise has converted the silent and unfrequented vale into the gay resort of fashion, and the favoured retreat of the invalid'.

BOURNEMOUTH, FROM EAST CLIFF 1904 52878

This view, with well-clad visitors strolling along the beach and sailing boats drawn up on the shore, shows a south coast beach before development. Even so, the trappings of a modern seaside resort were starting to appear. Bournemouth's first bathers were a mixture of the prudish and the daring. One early visitor reported that the shy paddlers 'bob about from dell to dell as if they thought that every bush concealed a serpent or a tempting apple'.

BOURNEMOUTH, THE PIER 1918 68064

Eugenius Birch, the grand master of Victorian pier building, created this pier (above) in 1880. It was iron-built, 838 feet long and 35 feet wide for its main span, leading to a pier-head 110 feet wide at the seaward end. This had a pavilion on top and landing stages for paddle-steamers at the sides. Birchmore and London's Pierrots performed in their tent 'three times daily'. There are few men in this photograph, taken in the last summer of the First World War, although Bournemouth was a popular retreat for men on leave from the trenches.

Did You Know?
BOURNEMOUTH
A MISCELLANY

"Bournemouth is one of the few English towns that one can safely call 'her'." (John Betjeman, 'First and Last Loves'.)

The Victorians developed the idea of building with glass to the furthest possible extent. The Winter Gardens building was erected in 1875 as the town's first large entertainment venue, and was home to Bournemouth's municipal orchestra. The famous composers Elgar, Sibelius and Holst all conducted here. The building was demolished in 1935.

BOURNEMOUTH, THE WINTER GARDENS c1875 8089

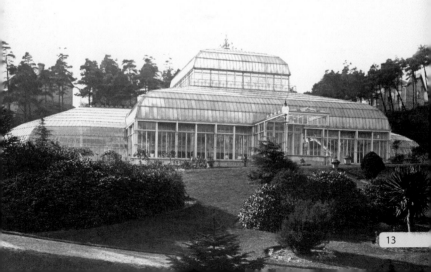

13

Bournemouth's pier was extended in 1894 and 1905, by which time its length had grown to 1,000 feet. The structure contained a lengthy landing stage, popular with steamers travelling along the south coast. 10,000 people landed on the pier on one Bank Holiday weekend in 1901.

Southbourne has an unfortunate place in history as the scene of the air crash that killed the pioneer pilot Mr Rolls, of Rolls Royce fame, in 1910. Rolls was the first person to die in a British air accident when his plane broke up in mid-air and crashed to the ground, in front of a crowd of several thousand. The downlands above the cliffs were popular with early aviators until Southbourne became too built up.

Shopkeepers were not slow in seeing the business potential of the wealthy and fashionable clientele that was attracted to Bournemouth. This arcade (right) is an impressive example of Victorian architecture. Bournemouth attracted a wealthy and fashionable clientele. The shopping arcade was very much a Victorian concept, enabling shoppers to browse without getting wet on rainy days.

A lot of effort was made to tame the wild landscape across which Bournemouth grew up. The Square stands astride the Bourne Stream, which was rapidly transformed into an attractive water feature forming the centre point of the resort. Since its early days Bournemouth has striven to be 'the Garden City by the Sea', and its lovely flower displays are a famous attraction for visitors.

BOURNEMOUTH, THE ARCADE c1955 B163153

BOURNEMOUTH, THE ARCADE c1871 5511

In its early days, Bournemouth's planners sought the advice and endorsement of Dr Granville, a connoisseur of favoured watering places and eventual author of 'Spas of England and Principal Sea-Bathing Places'. Granville announced that the resort was superb for the treatment of consumption, but urged them not to allow the new town to go downmarket. The resulting resort attracted fashionable, well-heeled visitors: hotel advertisements of the 1890s boasted of the patronage of the Prince of Wales (later Edward VII), the Empress of Austria, the King of the Belgians, Empress Eugenie of France, and 'all the leading Personages'.

The rapid expansion of Bournemouth can be measured by population figures: in 1851 the population was 692; by 1900 it had risen to 59,000.

The fine tower and spire of St Peter's Church dominated much of central Bournemouth, until planners allowed the construction of a number of large buildings nearby. The church was designed by the celebrated Victorian architect George Edmund Street, who also planned London's Law Courts (see page 48).

The attractive building at the pier entrance, seen below, which included a clock tower, no longer exists. At this part of the pier today is a two-storey octagonal leisure complex, incorporating shops, kiosks, show-bars and a multi-purpose hall. Costing £1.7million, it opened in 1981.

BOURNEMOUTH, THE PIER ENTRANCE 1900 45213

This fine skyline view of Edwardian Bournemouth, with its wealth of splendid church buildings, is a testimony to the endeavours of Bournemouth's first vicar, Alexander Morden Bennett, who

devoted much of his life to the promotion of Christianity in the resort, and to his son, Alexander Sykes Bennett, who carried on his father's good works.

BOURNEMOUTH, GENERAL VIEW 1904 52873

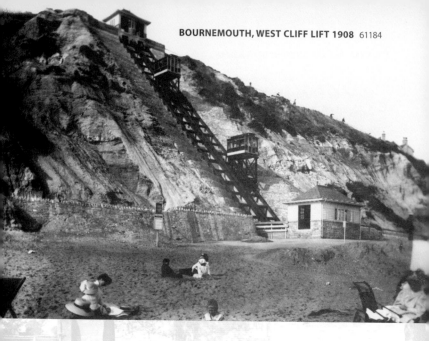

Cliff lifts became a popular solution to the problems of beach access in the later years of the Victorian period, and were used at a number of seaside resorts. The West Cliff Lift (above) may not have had to cope with the long gradient of some others, but was a masterpiece of mechanical design nevertheless.

Many of the trees in Bournemouth's various pleasure gardens were planted in Victorian times to 'improve the air quality', on the advice of the influential Dr Granville. True or not, the belief that the many pine trees in the area help to promote a relaxing atmosphere is still current today.

The Bournemouth Daily Echo is the town's evening newspaper, founded in 1900. Unlike many similar newspapers, it has survived to the present day at its Richmond Hill offices.

Nude bathing in Bournemouth was commonplace until late into the 19th century. However, one tourist, William Miller, was more outraged by the behaviour of the bystanders than by the immodesty of the bathers, commenting that 'the forwardness of the women makes it unpleasant for the bathers. For not content with gazing down from the cliffs above, they are often passing by or near the bathers. I think the visitors to Bournemouth are more shameless than at any other place'.

The present town hall was once the Mont Dore Hotel, one of the first places in England to have a telephone - the number was '3'.

BOURNEMOUTH, THE GARDENS AND THE MONT DORE HOTEL 1897 40563

The Pavilion Theatre and Ballroom was established in 1928, and has remained popular with visitors ever since. There are now several other venues for live entertainment in the town. The newer Bournemouth International Centre (the BIC), with its 3,500 capacity auditorium, has made Bournemouth the entertainment capital of the south coast, and a favourite venue for conferences.

Before Bournemouth was developed, the heathland and coastline of the area was much used by smugglers. The tower of St Andrew's Church at Kinson was used for storing contraband, and ledges on the tower have been damaged by the hauling up of kegs with ropes. In the churchyard is the grave of Robert Trotman, a smuggler shot dead by the customs officers in 1765. Ensbury Vicarage and Kinson House are also said to have connections with smugglers.

Lillie Langtry (1853-1929), the mistress of the Prince of Wales (later King Edward VII), lived for several years in Bournemouth, at the Red House on the East Cliff, which the Prince had specially built for her. The house in Derby Road is now the Langtry Manor Hotel and restaurant. The hotel displays portraits of Edward and his 'Jersey Lily', and features a tiny hatch high on the wall in the dining room from where the Prince of Wales inspected his guests before joining them for dinner. Embossed into the dining room fireplace are Lillie's initials, E L L.

The eminent 19th-century politician and Prime Minister William Gladstone was such a frequent visitor to Bournemouth that it was said, after he died, that you could not imagine society without him. He is commemorated in the area by a Gladstone suite in the Royal Bath Hotel, a Gladstone room in the Langtry Manor Hotel, Gladstone Road in Boscombe, and Gladstone Close in Christchurch.

KINSON, ST ANDREW'S CHURCH 1955 K115010

BOURNEMOUTH, THE SQUARE 1923 74782

By the 1920s Bournemouth had become a major south coast resort, rivalling Brighton and Torquay. The traffic in the Square increased accordingly, with private motorcars competing with the charabanc for parking spaces. The latter would take trippers to the many beautiful localities nearby, such as the Isle of Purbeck and the New Forest.

During the Second World War Bournemouth was not a target in itself for enemy bombing raids, but was unfortunately on the route of raids to other places in the country. It was not unknown for the German bombers to jettison unused bombs on the town, and 219 local people were killed by enemy action.

The 1st Earl of Malmesbury commented on the smuggling trade of the Bourne Heath: 'All classes contributed to its support, the farmers lent their teams and labourers, and the gentry openly connived at the practise and dealt with the smugglers. The cargoes, chiefly of brandy, were usually concealed in furze bushe that extended from Ringwood to Poole, and in the New Forest for thirty miles'.

Since this part of the coast had few harbours, most of the coastal pleasure boats moored alongside Bournemouth's piers. In the photograph below we see the Swanage paddle-steamer about to set off.

BOURNEMOUTH, THE SWANAGE BOAT 1908 61183

While Bournemouth grew up in Victorian times, the village of Holdenhurst on its outskirts is an ancient farming settlement, mentioned in the Domesday survey of 1086 as 'Holeest'. The word comes from the old English 'holegn' or 'holly', while 'hyrst' means copse. The white stones around the village green and the stripes at the foot of the lamppost in this photograph may

have been visual aids during the wartime blackout. Just visible behind the thatched cottage in the centre of the photograph is the roof of a low, thatched half-timbered building, believed to be the oldest in Holdenhurst. It is referred to in an old deed as the Hospice of St Mary Magdalene, but locals called it the Leper Hospital, which it may have been in former times.

HOLDENHURST, THE VILLAGE GREEN c1945 H296007

BOURNEMOUTH, PAVILION GARDENS c1955
B163154

The Russell-Cotes Art Gallery and Museum on Russell-Cotes Road specialises in Victoriana. The building itself is a wonderful example of Victorian architecture, with a pinnacled roof. The house, East Cliff Hall, was left to the town by Sir Merton Russell-Cotes and his wife, along with their art gallery and collection of items picked up in their travels all over the world. The museum also has a collection of theatrical items relating to the great 19th-century actor Sir Henry Irving. Sir Merton and his wife Annie loved Bournemouth, and were tireless in their promotion of the resort.

'Bournemouth!
How shall I sing thy praise, fair favoured spot,
That nestles 'mid thy hills and silvery groves
Of fragrant pines? From out thy dense alcoves,
Bright villas peep – 't has been my happy lot
To dwell amid thy shady nooks, I wot,
Through many winters.'
(Sir Merton Russell-Cotes)

John Galsworthy (1867-1933), the author of 'The Forsyte Saga', went to school at Saugeen Primary School for Boys, Derby Road, Bournemouth, and also sang in the choir at nearby St Swithun's Church.

Bournemouth had the first indoor bowling green in the country. It was built on the site of the first Winter Gardens when that building was demolished in 1935 (see photo 8089 on page 13). After the Second World War the bowling green building was found to have excellent acoustic qualities and was turned into an entertainment venue, the 'new' Winter Gardens, home of the Bournemouth Symphony Orchestra. The site is currently (2005) awaiting further redevelopment.

One of Bournemouth's more colourful characters was Chang Woo Gow (1846-1893), the 'Chinese Giant', who weighed 26 stone and was 8 feet tall. He was born in Foochow, China, but toured the world for 25 years as a 'curiosity'. He came to Bournemouth as it was thought that he was suffering from tuberculosis, and was a great attraction at civic functions, appearing in Chinese costume. Chang married an Australian woman and they settled in Bournemouth, in a house called 'Moyuen' in Southcote Road. They opened a Chinese tearoom, but Chang's wife died in 1893. Chang was devastated by grief and died four months later; he was buried in Bournemouth Cemetery.

For a short time after the end of the First World War there was a 'water aerodrome' to the south of Bournemouth Pier. Supermarine Aviation operated summer flying boat services from Bournemouth to Southampton and the Isle of Wight.

BOURNEMOUTH, THE METROPOLE
HOTEL 1900 45227

BOURNEMOUTH, THE PIER APPROACH c1955 B163012

The epitaph on the tomb of the smuggler Robert Trotman, in the graveyard of St Andrew's Church, Kinson, Bournemouth reads:

> *To the Memory of ROBERT TROTMAN*
> *Late of Rond [ie Rowde] in the County*
> *Of Wilts who was barbarously*
> *Murder'd on the Shore near*
> *Poole the 24 March 1765*

> *A little Tea one leaf I did not steal*
> *For Guiltless Blood shed I to GOD appeal*
> *Put Tea in one scale human Blood in tother*
> *And think what tis to slay thy harmless Brother*

In 1898 Bournemouth played a part in the experiments of the radio pioneer Guglielmo Marconi (1874-1937). Marconi set up a transmitting station at the Madeira Hotel on Bournemouth's West Cliff, with the intention of transmitting between there and the transmitter he had established on the Isle of Wight. Very soon Marconi fell out with the management of the Madeira Hotel and moved his equipment to a nearby house called Sandhills. From here he used a 125-foot mast to exchange messages with the Isle of Wight station and vessels in Poole Bay and the Solent. The world's first paid-for radiogram, transmitted from the Isle of Wight, was received at Sandhills on 3 June 1898.

BOURNEMOUTH, THE PIER 1908 61180

WESTBOURNE, COUNTY GATES 1913 66144

County Gates stood on the old boundary between
Dorset and Hampshire, which now marks the
boundary between Bournemouth and Poole. The area
is now a roundabout at the end of the Wessex Way.

BOURNEMOUTH, THE PIER ENTRANCE 1925 78768

Two benefactresses in the Bournemouth area were sisters Georgina
and Marianne Talbot, the founders of Talbot Village. When they
moved to the area from London in 1842 the sisters (particularly
Georgina) were shocked at the poverty of the local working families,
and bought 465 acres of land from Sir George Tapps-Gervis to create
a self-sufficient village to enable unemployed workers to support
themselves and their families by their own efforts. Talbot Village
comprised of six farms and 16 cottages, each with an acre of land, a
pigsty and a well. In 1862 Georgina also organised the building of
seven almshouses and a village school.

The Edgar Wallace film 'To Have and to Hold' (1963) was shot in Bournemouth. Apparently the producer, Jack Greenwood, went on honeymoon in Bournemouth and liked the town.

Bournemouth International Airport began life as RAF Hurn in 1941, accommodating a wide variety of RAF units. It was handed over to the Ministry of Civil Aviation in 1944. Hurn was the main terminus for international flights into the UK until Heathrow opened for business in 1949. The airport was purchased by the Bournemouth Corporation and Dorset County Council in 1969, and it was run by them as Bournemouth Airport (becoming Bournemouth International Airport) until 1995, when it was sold to National Express.

SOUTHBOURNE, THE RAVINE 1922 72718

37

BOURNEMOUTH

A MISCELLANY

Did You Know?

The site of Bournemouth University was once occupied by a flying training school operated by the Bournemouth Aviation Company. Set up in November 1915, this was a school for training pilots during the First World War, and closed down in 1917. A civil flying

BOURNEMOUTH, ALUM CHINE 1925 78781

school was also set up by the Bournemouth Aviation Company at Ensbury Park in 1916, but a series of accidents led to its closure in 1928. The site is now covered by housing.

SPORTING BOURNEMOUTH

The financial problems that troubled AFC Bournemouth in the mid 1990s led them to become pioneers, as Europe's first professional 'community club'. A trust fund set up by supporters took over the club on 18 June 1997, with the club 15 minutes from closure. Within five years the club was playing in its own stadium.

One of the most colourful sporting figures from the Bournemouth area was boxer Freddie Mills, born in Parkstone in 1919. A top-class boxer, he was World Light Heavyweight Champion from 1947 to 1950. His career after boxing was also eventful, as he became a London nightclub owner, and associate of the Krays. He met a tragic end, found shot dead in Soho in 1965. The police said his death was suicide, but a number of lurid theories appeared, including one that suggested Chinese gangsters were after his nightclub.

Bournemouth once had a racecourse at Ensbury Park, which staged horseracing between the two world wars. Today there is little sign that it ever existed.

Bournemouth-born tennis star Virginia Wade is of course most famous for her triumph in the women's singles at Wimbledon in 1977, the silver jubilee year of Queen Elizabeth II, but she had a long and distinguished tennis career, and was responsible for two major 'firsts' in the sport. In 1968, before becoming professional, she won the first 'open' tennis competition, the British Hard Court Open at Bournemouth; as an amateur she had to refuse the prize money. She later won the first US Open tournament, beating Billie Jean King in the final. Off the court, another 'first' was in 1982, when she became the first woman to be elected to the Wimbledon committee.

QUIZ QUESTIONS

Answers on page 49.

1. What happened to Bournemouth's pier during the Second World War?

2. Which fictional heroine murdered her seducer in a Bournemouth boarding house?

3. Which unimpressed visitor to Bournemouth said that life there 'was as monotonous as a weevil's in a biscuit'?

4. Who promoted Bournemouth with the words: 'Never say see Naples and Die; rather see Bournemouth and Live!'?

5. Who described Bournemouth as a 'Mediterranean lounging place on the English Channel'?

6. When Mark Cox beat Pancho Gonzales in the Bournemouth Hardcourt Tennis Championship in 1968, what was significant about the achievement?

7. Why does the name 'Portman' occur in various parts of Bournemouth, such as the Portman Ravine at Southbourne?

8. Bournemouth's war memorial in Central Gardens is guarded by what?

9. What was the name of the famous smuggling leader in the Bournemouth area, who claimed never to have killed a man in the course of his career?

10. Which TV sitcom was filmed in Bournemouth?

BOURNEMOUTH, FROM SOUTHBOURNE TERRACE c1870 5500

43

RECIPE

DORSET SAUSAGE

Thomas Hardy used Bournemouth for several scenes in his novels, thinly disguised as 'Sandbourne'. This recipe for Dorset sausage (Bournemouth has been in Dorset since 1974) is Mrs Thomas Hardy's own, and would have been served to the author and visitors at the Hardy home near Dorchester.

Ingredients:

1lb/450g minced beef

1lb/450g minced ham

8oz/225g fresh breadcrumbs

1 small nutmeg, grated

Half a teaspoon ground mace

2 eggs, beaten

salt and pepper

Mix the meats together, then add the breadcrumbs and mix again. Stir in the eggs and seasonings, and either put into a large damp cloth and tie securely, then boil in water to cover for 3 hours, or bake in a greased cake tin for about 1½ hours. Leave to cool completely before turning out, and scatter with toasted breadcrumbs. This is like a coarse terrine, and is eaten cold, in slices - ideal for a picnic.

BOURNEMOUTH, EAST CLIFF 1918 68069

BOURNEMOUTH, THE BEACH 1904 52880

RECIPE

STUFFED MACKEREL
WITH GOOSEBERRY SAUCE

Before the development of the Bourne Heath as a holiday resort in the early 19th century, one of the main occupations of the few people living in the area would have been mackerel fishing. Gooseberries have long been a traditional accompaniment to mackerel in English cookery.

Ingredients:
4 mackerel, gutted and de-scaled
1 tablespoon chopped parsley
1 tablespoon chopped thyme
Half a teaspoon grated lemon rind
1 tablespoon lemon juice
1oz/25g soft white breadcrumbs
Seasoned flour
8oz/225g gooseberries
Sugar to taste

Wash and dry the mackerel, and clean them. Mix the parsley, thyme, lemon rind, lemon juice and soft breadcrumbs and stuff the mackerel with this mixture. Roll the fish lightly in seasoned flour. Melt a little butter or oil in a baking pan and, when it is very hot, put in the mackerel. Put into the oven and bake at 350 degrees F, 180 degrees C, gas mark 4, for 25 minutes, carefully turning fish over halfway through.

Meanwhile, for the gooseberry sauce, simmer the gooseberries in very little water until they are soft. Rub them through a sieve and sweeten lightly. Warm the gooseberry sauce through before serving with the mackerel.

BOURNEMOUTH, ST PETER'S
CHURCH 1887 19561

QUIZ ANSWERS

1. Its central supports and decking were demolished in 1940 by the Royal Engineers to prevent the possibility of the pier being used by a German invasion force.

2. In Thomas Hardy's 'Tess of the d'Urbervilles', Tess murders her seducer, Alec, in a boarding house in Bournemouth (Hardy called it 'Sandbourne) before running away with her true love, and estranged husband, Angel Clare.

3. The author Robert Louis Stevenson. He was staying in Bournemouth for the good of his health, which had been ruined, in part, by the excesses of his riotous early life in Edinburgh.

4. Sir Merton Russell-Cotes and his wife Annie. Sir Merton wrote: 'When I first came to Bournemouth it was terra incognita, and I determined to make it the talk of Europe'. Lady Russell-Cotes was popularly known as 'the Queen of Bournemouth'.

5. Thomas Hardy.

6. It was the first time that an amateur player had beaten a professional in an open tournament.

7. Portman was the maiden name of Henrietta, the second wife of Captain Lewis Tregonwell, known as 'the founder of Bournemouth'.

8. The war memorial is guarded by four stone lions.

9. Isaac Gulliver. His favourite landing places were at Branksome Chine, Canford Cliffs and Bourne Heath, moving goods inland through Pug's Hole to Talbot Woods. One legend about Gulliver tells how, when his house in Kinson was searched, he dusted his face with chalk and lay in a coffin, pretending to be dead.

10. The house and street scenes from the TV series 'One Foot In the Grave' were filmed in Bournemouth.

BOURNEMOUTH, THE GARDENS 1904 52877

FRANCIS FRITH

PIONEER VICTORIAN PHOTOGRAPHER

Francis Frith, founder of the world-famous photographic archive, was a complex and multi-talented man. A devout Quaker and a highly successful Victorian businessman, he was philosophical by nature and pioneering in outlook. By 1855 he had already established a wholesale grocery business in Liverpool, and sold it for the astonishing sum of £200,000, which is the equivalent today of over £15,000,000. Now in his thirties, and captivated by the new science of photography, Frith set out on a series of pioneering journeys up the Nile and to the Near East.

INTRIGUE AND EXPLORATION

He was the first photographer to venture beyond the sixth cataract of the Nile. Africa was still the mysterious 'Dark Continent', and Stanley and Livingstone's historic meeting was a decade into the future. The conditions for picture taking confound belief. He laboured for hours in his wicker dark-room in the sweltering heat of the desert, while the volatile chemicals fizzed dangerously in their trays. Back in London he exhibited his photographs and was 'rapturously cheered' by members of the Royal Society. His reputation as a photographer was made overnight.

VENTURE OF A LIFE-TIME

By the 1870s the railways had threaded their way across the country, and Bank Holidays and half-day Saturdays had been made obligatory by Act of Parliament. All of a sudden the working man and his family were able to enjoy days out, take holidays, and see a little more of the world.

With typical business acumen, Francis Frith foresaw that these new tourists would enjoy having souvenirs to commemorate their days out. For the next thirty years he travelled the country by train and by pony and trap, producing fine photographs of seaside resorts and beauty spots that were keenly bought by millions of Victorians. These prints were painstakingly pasted into family albums and pored over during the dark nights of winter, rekindling precious memories of summer excursions. Frith's studio was soon supplying retail shops all over the country, and by 1890 F Frith & Co had become the greatest specialist photographic publishing company in the world, with over 2,000 sales outlets, and pioneered the picture postcard.

FRANCIS FRITH'S LEGACY

Francis Frith had died in 1898 at his villa in Cannes, his great project still growing. By 1970 the archive he created contained over a third of a million pictures showing 7,000 British towns and villages.

Frith's legacy to us today is of immense significance and value, for the magnificent archive of evocative photographs he created provides a unique record of change in the cities, towns and villages throughout Britain over a century and more. Frith and his fellow studio photographers revisited locations many times down the years to update their views, compiling for us an enthralling and colourful pageant of British life and character.

We are fortunate that Frith was dedicated to recording the minutiae of everyday life. For it is this sheer wealth of visual data, the painstaking chronicle of changes in dress, transport, street layouts, buildings, housing and landscape that captivates us so much today, offering us a powerful link with the past and with the lives of our ancestors.

Computers have now made it possible for Frith's many thousands of images to be accessed almost instantly. The archive offers every one of us an opportunity to examine the places where we and our families have lived and worked down the years. Its images, depicting our shared past, are now bringing pleasure and enlightenment to millions around the world a century and more after his death.

For further information visit: www.francisfrith.com

INTERIOR DECORATION

Frith's photographs can be seen framed and as giant wall murals in thousands of pubs, restaurants, hotels, banks, retail stores and other public buildings throughout Britain. These provide interesting and attractive décor, generating strong local interest and acting as a powerful reminder of gentler days in our increasingly busy and frenetic world.

FRITH PRODUCTS

All Frith photographs are available as prints and posters in a variety of different sizes and styles. In the UK we also offer a range of other gift and stationery products illustrated with Frith photographs, although many of these are not available for delivery outside the UK – see our web site for more information on the products available for delivery in your country.

THE INTERNET

Over 100,000 photographs of Britain can be viewed and purchased on the Frith web site. The web site also includes memories and reminiscences contributed by our customers, who have personal knowledge of localities and of the people and properties depicted in Frith photographs. If you wish to learn more about a specific town or village you may find these reminiscences fascinating to browse. Why not add your own comments if you think they would be of interest to others? See **www.francisfrith.com**

PLEASE HELP US BRING FRITH'S PHOTOGRAPHS TO LIFE

Our authors do their best to recount the history of the places they write about. They give insights into how particular towns and villages developed, they describe the architecture of streets and buildings, and they discuss the lives of famous people who lived there. But however knowledgeable our authors are, the story they tell is necessarily incomplete.

Frith's photographs are so much more than plain historical documents. They are living proofs of the flow of human life down the generations. They show real people at real moments in history; and each of those people is the son or daughter of someone, the brother or sister, aunt or uncle, grandfather or grandmother of someone else. All of them lived, worked and played in the streets depicted in Frith's photographs.

We would be grateful if you would give us your insights into the places shown in our photographs: the streets and buildings, the shops, businesses and industries. Post your memories of life in those streets on the Frith website: what it was like growing up there, who ran the local shop and what shopping was like years ago; if your workplace is shown tell us about your working day and what the building is used for now. Read other visitors' memories and reconnect with your shared local history and heritage. With your help more and more Frith photographs can be brought to life, and vital memories preserved for posterity, and for the benefit of historians in the future.

Wherever possible, we will try to include some of your comments in future editions of our books. Moreover, if you spot errors in dates, titles or other facts, please let us know, because our archive records are not always completely accurate—they rely on 140 years of human endeavour and hand-compiled records. You can email us using the contact form on the website.

Thank you!

For further information, trade, or author enquiries
please contact us at the address below:

**The Francis Frith Collection, Oakley Business Park,
Wylye Road, Dinton, Wiltshire SP3 5EU.**
Tel: +44 (0)1722 716 376 Fax: +44 (0)1722 716 881
e-mail: sales@francisfrith.co.uk **www.francisfrith.com**